Embroidery Beading
DESIGNS AND TECHNIQUES

Plate 1 *A vintage evening bag from the 1800s worked with black, silver and white crystal beads, and fringed with cut jet*

Embroidery Beading

DESIGNS AND TECHNIQUES

Maisie Jarratt

Kangaroo Press

Acknowledgments

My thanks to those who have helped me in compiling this book—
for photography, Tim Wade of Pennant Hills; for typing, Debra Moore of Gerringong;
and for overall support, my husband Duncan Jarratt.

First published in Australia in 1992 by Kangaroo Press
an imprint of Simon & Schuster (Australia) Pty Limited
20 Barcoo Street, East Roseville NSW 2069
Reprinted in paperback 1995

A Viacom Company
Sydney New York London Toronto Tokyo Singapore

ISBN 0 86417 720 8

Printed in Hong Kong through Colorcraft Ltd

10 9 8 7 6 5 4 3 2

Contents

Introduction

This book is intended to follow on from my first book, *How to Bead*, also published by Kangaroo Press, in which the methods and techniques of embroidery beading are explained. It presents exciting designs based on combinations of these basic techniques, which take on a new look in a different context, and with different beads and colours.

Some of the designs use the more advanced techniques such as tambour or French frame beading, but quite a number are very simple to embroider if the instructions are followed carefully. Some are very inexpensive to bead, and an expensive-looking garment can be created for only a small outlay.

In the last few years there has been a considerable revival of interest in beading, and the variety of methods of this craft should provide hours of pleasure for people of all ages.

A brief history

The bead must be one of humanity's earliest artefacts. In as primitive a form as a piece of shell or an acorn, it was most likely fashioned to satisfy the basic need for personal adornment. From this simple beginning the bead has been formed from nearly every material known, and used as a basis for barter, trade and currency, as well as an ornament. In addition, strung beads have a more utilitarian purpose when used, even to this day, as a counting device, whether for practical purposes as in the abacus or for religious purposes as a guide to prayers, as in the rosary.

In the ancient tombs of Egypt, brightly coloured beads of various shapes in glass, ceramics, gold and coral can be found in elaborate assemblages, representing one of the richest periods of bead ornamentation.

Since the fourteenth century, Venice has been one of the main centres for bead production, although in recent times Czechoslovakia has gained the reputation for producing some of the finest glass beads.

Beadwork skills reached new heights in the seventeenth century with elaborate beaded purses, and in the eighteenth century when lighter fabrics were introduced.

In the 1920s beadwork became a necessary part of fashion, and flapper dresses and evening bags were elaborately decorated with beads, which generally outlived the items they adorned.

The current revival in beadworking embraces many different methods, some of which are of historical as well as technical interest.

Methods

Tracing a design

1. Sketch out the design you wish to embroider on tracing paper with firm, bold lines, and transfer it to the fabric, using a fade-away pencil.
2. It is a good idea to run a tacking thread around the design. If the pencil fades away while you are working the design the thread saves a lot of retracing. The thread can be pulled out when the beading is completed.
3. Collect the different beads and sequins needed for the design before you start.
4. If you are uncertain of your bead choices, sew a few beads and sequins onto a small sample of the fabric to see how they suit the design and the material.

Washing instructions

1. Hand wash in cold water with Softly or a wool wash.
2. Rinse, and drip dry in the shade.
3. Iron on the wrong side of the garment with the beading resting on a towel—press on a warm iron setting only.
4. *Do not* wash in a machine or tumble dry.

Remember

1. The flow of the work is in general from right to left, and always towards you. Left handed people work in the opposite direction, but the principles remain the same.
2. Always use double-threaded cotton, knotted at the end, when sewing on beads, sequins and stones.
3. Wherever the type of stitch to be used has not been stipulated, use a whip stitch, sewing in a right to left movement.

   Bugle beads are usually sewn with a back stitch, but whip stitch is also used.
4. The large central bead of a flower spray should always be stitched twice.
5. Practice your intended method of beading on a sample of the fabric you will be working on before you begin.
6. Be gentle with the fabric you are working on, and do not stretch it. This especially applies to jersey. Stretched material bounces back when tension is released and puckers up the beadwork.
7. As with all sewing, wash your hands before you start.

Materials and equipment required for beading—beads may come loose in packets, or strung together in long lengths. The cornaly needles at bottom right are used for tambour (French frame) beading

Plate 2 *Hedge roses worked on a pullover (page 26)*

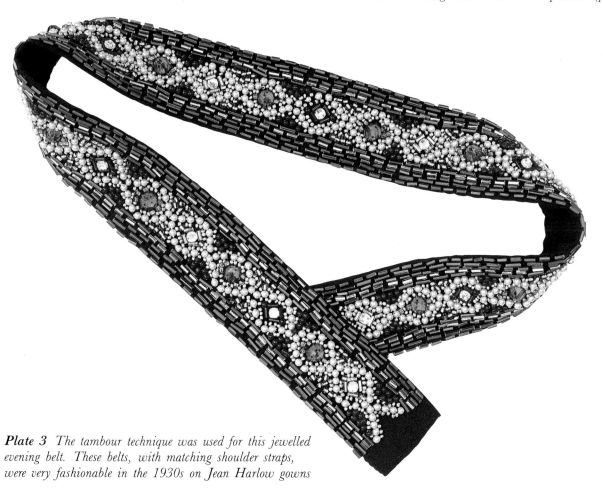

Plate 3 *The tambour technique was used for this jewelled evening belt. These belts, with matching shoulder straps, were very fashionable in the 1930s on Jean Harlow gowns*

Plate 4 *Bow motif (page 13)*

Plate 5 *Paisley motifs
1 and 2 (page 15)*

Plate 6 *Knitted sweater embroidered with paisley
motifs (page 17)*

Plate 7 Fuchsia (page 20)

Plate 8 Split petal flowers, below (page 22)

Designs for clothes and pictures

Bow

Plate 4   This beaded bow looks very effective on the front of a blouse or sweater.

dangling arrangements

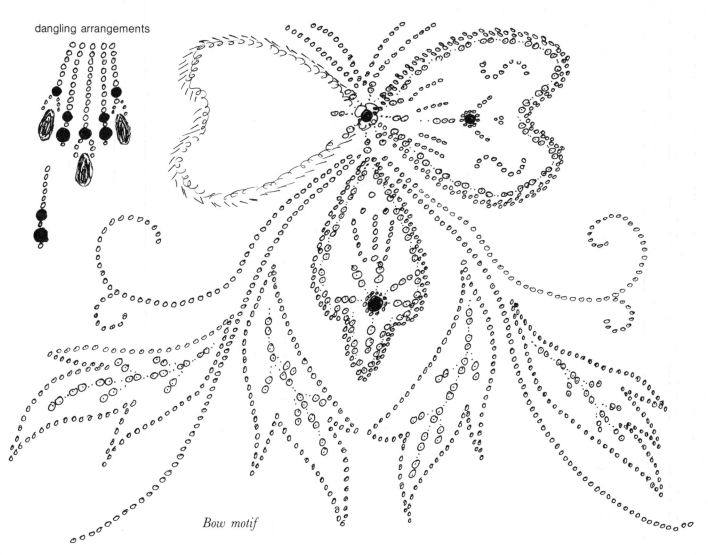

Bow motif

You will need

Cut crystal seed beads
Crystal iridescent cup sequins
Electric blue cup sequins
2 small rhinestones
2 rosemonties
5 pearls
5 matching cut beads or drops for the centre hanging arrangements

Method

1. Trace the design onto the fabric. Starting with the flower at the centre of the bow, sew a small rhinestone for the centre, at the same time sewing a tiny bead over the hole in the stone. Bring the needle up through the hole and thread 1 bead, then insert the needle back through the hole. This covers the thread.

   Thread 6 crystal seed beads together and sew in a looped fashion around the stone four times. (See sketch.)

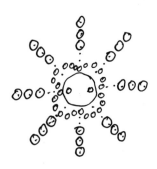

   Thread 3 crystal seed beads, 1 crystal sequin, 1 bead, 1 blue sequin, 1 bead, 1 blue sequin together eight times and sew outwards from the stone. Sew the next rhinestone on the lower part of the bow, making only half a flower. (See sketch.)

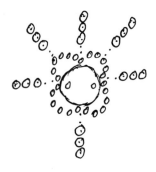

2. Using crystal seed beads, bead the outside line of the bow. Thread 3 beads together and sew with a whip stitch from right to left, giving an angled effect. Inside this line, thread together 3 beads, 1 crystal sequin, 1 bead, 1 blue sequin and sew with a whip stitch, remembering to sew right to left.

   Continue this way onto the lower section of the bow.

3. Return to the top section of the bow. Sew a rosemontie in the centre of each side of the bow, threading 3 beads together and sewing around the edge of the rosemontie four times. (*Always bead around stones.*)

   A few details have been added inside the bow to highlight it: some tiny swirls in 'S' shapes, short lines and a little cluster spotting of three beads;

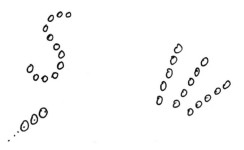

   also groups of 3 beads, 1 sequin, 1 bead, 1 sequin, 1 bead, 1 sequin threaded together. (See sketch.)

4. Add three beaded lines and some spotting above the half flower on the lower section of the bow. (See sketch.)

5. Bead the main stem of the leaves using blue chunky beads, sewn on one at a time. Outline the leaves with a single row of crystal beads, then sew single swirl lines of crystal beads to each side.

6. For the centre vein of the leaf, thread together 3 crystal seed beads, 1 crystal sequin, 1 bead, 1 blue sequin and sew these to the fabric eight times. Add side veins in the same manner. (See sketch.)

7. Sew the dangling arrangement from the main flower in the centre of the bow. For the centre drop, thread 12 crystal beads, 1 pearl, 3 beads, 1 drop, 3 beads; insert the needle back through the pearl and the 12 beads, giving a single string with a drop on the end. Repeat this twice. Thread 7 beads, 1 pearl, 3 beads, 1 cut blue bead, one bead and insert the needle back through the large bead, seed beads and pearl, leaving the seed bead on the end as an anchor. Repeat this once. Five drops in all. (See sketch.)

Paisley motifs 1 and 2

Plate 5

Beading on paisley designs should look very ornate.

You will need

Shot bronze seed beads
Chunky gold beads
Chunky bronze beads
Size 3 black bugle beads
Bronze cup sequins
Seed pearls
9 long pearls
8 oblong cut black beads
3 cut black beads

Method: motif 1

1. Trace design onto fabric, blouse or sweater. Sew single beads all around the outside line with whip stitch, from right to left. (See p.12 of *How to Bead*.) Bead the inside line using shot bronze seed beads. Thread 3 beads together and sew around beside the single beads of the outside line.
2. Along the centre line inside the large paisley, sew 1 pearl, 1 oblong cut black bead (in all 9 pearls and 8 black beads).

   With black bugle beads sew outwards at an angle to both sides of each pearl. Continue all along the centre line.

Paisley motif 1 — The second paisley motif is sketched on the next page

3. This section of the design has two small scrolls, each with a rosemontie sewn inside the curve. Below those stones, sew 3 bronze chunky beads in cluster spots. Still beading the inside section, sew the eleven tiny curved lines with single beads. (See sketch.)
4. On the outside, there are five curves marked. Bead each of these with bronze chunky beads, sewn singly onto the fabric. (See sketch.) Inside each curve, sew a pearl with 3 spots of bronze seed beads.
5. The three single-line scrolls are beaded using gold chunky beads sewn on singly. Where each large scroll has a tiny scroll to break the line, on the inside, thread 3 seed beads, 1 bronze sequin, 1 bead, 1 sequin, 1 bead, 1 sequin and sew outwards from the line of beads. Repeat this to each side of the first line omitting the last bead and sequin. Bead along the scroll sewing outwards, 1 long pearl, 1 black bugle bead, alternately to each side. (See sketch.)

Method: motif 2

1. Repeat the outline as given for the first paisley design. Beading on the centre line, thread 3 shot bronze seed beads, 1 bronze cup sequin and repeat 12 times.

   Halfway along this line sew pairs of black bugle beads and long pearls angling outwards, 4 times each side of the centre line. The small curves on the inside are sewn with bronze chunky beads.

   The scrolls are beaded as for the first motif.

Paisley motif 2

Paisley motif 3

Plate 6

This design looks very lovely beaded across the front of a cream double-knit sweater.

You will need

Size 2 shot green bugle beads
Shot green seed beads
Gold chunky beads
Size 1 9ct gold-lined bugle beads
Cream seed pearls
Shot green cup sequins
Crystal iridescent cup sequins
Rosemontie cut stones
4 topas cut drops

Method

1. Trace design onto fabric. The swirls and scrolls in the upper parts of the design can be trailed slightly over the shoulderlines of the garment.
2. Bead the two main paisley designs first. Thread 3 shot green seed beads together and sew from right to left with a whip stitch. This method is illustrated in *How To Bead* on p.13.

3. Sew size 1 gold bugle beads all around inside the outer line.
4. For the centre line, thread 3 shot green seed beads, 1 crystal iridescent sequin, 1 bead, 1 shot green sequin and sew together using a whip stitch. Continue along the centre line. This should give a raised effect, with the sequin combination adding extra sparkle.
5. On each side of the centre line, thread 4 green seed beads and sew together zigzag fashion.

Continue with this method along each side of the raised line.
  Sew a seed pearl into each inside vee.
6. The 5 swirls on the outside curve of the paisley are sewn with single beads. Inside each swirl sew a rosemontie stone with a single row of beads surrounding it. Spot a single bead three times. (See sketch.) Repeat with each swirl.

7. Moving to the stem trailing down from between the two main paisley designs, sew size 2 shot green bugle beads angling down the stem with a back stitch. The three swirls at the top of the stem are sewn with single beads from right to left, with a whip stitch.
  For the square-ended leaves, thread 3 beads, 1 crystal sequin, 1 bead, 1 shot green sequin and sew around the leaf, keeping the ends square.

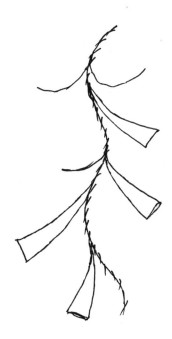

The diagram for this design appears over the page

Bring the two parts of the
design together at the
dotted lines

8. The swirls and scrolls in the upper part of the design are sewn with single size 2 shot green bugle beads, using a back stitch. Bead the centre stem first. On the outside curve of each swirl and scroll sew size 1 gold bugle beads, next to the green beads. (See sketch.)

9. Finally, sew the sprays of 3 swirls with size 2 bugle beads, using a back stitch. Add a spotting of single gold chunky beads. Mark each dot with a pencil as this will make them easier to work. Insert your needle from spot to spot ensuring that the fabric does not pucker.

10. Work the last two scrolls in the same manner as the others.

11. To bead the tiny vees, thread 3 shot green seed beads, 1 crystal iridescent sequin, 1 bead, 1 shot green sequin, 1 bead, 1 sequin, 1 bead, 1 sequin and sew outwards. Repeat this to make a vee leaving enough space to sew the cut topas drop in the centre. Sew it with double thread 3 times as it is glass and could cut through the thread.

Fuchsia

Plate 7

You will need

Crystal iridescent mauve cup sequins
Shot mauve solid cup sequins
Lilac iridescent cup sequins
Purple cup sequins
Mauve iridescent chunky beads
5 mauve pearls or glass beads for the hanging stamen of the flower
Size 2 green bugle beads for the stems and leaves

Method

1. Trace the design onto the fabric, making sure you mark the lines on the flower and bud where the beads are to be sewn (this is important to capture the petticoat look of the flower). Bead all these lines first using mauve thread and chunky beads, sewn one at a time.
2. For the centre section between the lines of beads, using mauve thread, alternate mauve and lilac sequins to give a variegated effect.
3. Sequin each side of the centre section alternating lighter and darker shdes, using four colours in all, i.e. lilac, purple, crystal mauve and shot mauve. The scalloped inside edge of the bell should be mainly purple with a few lilac sequins mixed in.
4. The top recurved flower petals are sequinned in four colours: start by alternating the darker colours, and about 2 cm out from the centre graduate to the paler colours, progressing to the tips of the petals. (See plate 00.)
5. For the hanging stamens thread 12 mauve chunky beads, 1 pearl, 1 bead onto a single string, and insert the needle back to the edge of the flower leaving the end bead to anchor. Continue this way omitting 2 beads each time on subsequent pairs of stamens, working 5 in all.
6. Bead the two lines marked inside the bud with mauve chunky beads. The centre of the bud is sequinned in the two pale colours alternated, with the darker shades added in along the outside edge. To shape the top of the bud where it joins the stem, add a few beads.

7. Bead the stems and leaves using size 2 green bugle beads. If desired, lilac or purple colours can be used for this to keep the motif all one colour. Sew bugle beads with a back stitch along the stem, so they lie neatly at an angle. The edges of the leaves are beaded with a single line of the Size 2 bugle beads, sewn with a whip stitch from right to left, creating a picot effect. Bugle beads are then added for the veins. (See sketch.)

Split petal flowers

Plate 8

This is a very dainty design: broken scrolls with a pretty split petal flower. It is a very simple design for beginners to bead. The split petal flower technique can be found on p.21 of *How To Bead*.

You will need

Pale pink seed beads (or colour desired)
Iridescent cup sequins
Rosemontie stones

Method

1. Trace the design onto the fabric. Mark 5 strokes for each flower to represent the petals. Sew a rosemontie for the centre of the flower. Thread 5 beads together and sew these 4 times in a looped fashion around the stone, so that they stand up around it.

   To make a looped petal, bring the needle through beside the centre stone. Thread 7 beads together, laying them flat from the centre stone, and make a small stitch to anchor. Thread 7 more beads and bring these back to the centre stone.

Bring the two parts of the design together at the dotted lines

Split petal flowers

Insert the needle halfway between these two rows of beads and thread 5 beads. Re-insert the needle just above the two lines of beads, splitting the section to form a petal. Repeat this 4 times.

2. Bead the connecting scrolls and swirls with groups of 3 beads threaded together, sewn from right to left. The small swirls emerging from between the flower petals are also beaded with 3 beads together, like the larger scrolls. A tiny sequin flower can be added to the ends of these swirls, or 5 claw-shaped lines can be beaded to form a flower.

3. To work the leaves, starting from the top point of the leaf, thread 3 beads, 1 sequin, 1 bead, 1 sequin together, and repeat this sequence sewing zigzag fashion. (See sketch.)

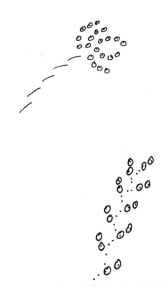

leaf beading, sew outward

Wisteria

Plate 9

To capture the effect of the hanging wisteria flower, a variety of iridescent crystal, mauve, lilac and purple beads and sequins is used. This is not an easy flower to bead.

You will need

Crystal iridescent cup sequins
Pale mauve shot solid cup sequins
Lilac crystal iridescent cup sequins
Purple solid cup sequins
Lilac sequins with the hole on the edge
Pale mauve iridescent chunky beads
Size 2 green bugle beads
Green seed beads

Method

1. Trace the design onto the fabric. Work the main flower stem with green seed beads, sewn singly with a whip stitch, from right to left. Bead the short stalks which alternate along the main stem. (See sketch.) These are the points of attachment for the small flowers.
2. Use mauve thread for the beads and sequins of the petals. All the petals are beaded in a raised fashion, sewn from each side of the short stalks that have already been beaded.

    Thread together 2 chunky mauve beads, 1 crystal cup sequin, 1 mauve solid sequin. Work this twice to each side of the stalk. To finish the small flower, thread 2 mauve chunky beads, 1 crystal sequin, 1 lilac sequin, 1 purple sequin, and sew these together into the hole of the large lilac sequin with the hole on the edge. Continue in this fashion, graduating to the end of the stem. (See sketch.)
3. Using size 2 green bugle beads sewn with a back stitch, work the leaf stems. Use green seed beads to outline the leaves. For the centre vein on the leaves, work with 3 beads threaded together, and sew bugle beads angling outwards to each side.

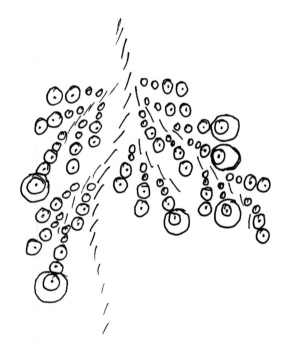

Wisteria

Hedge roses

Plate 2

You will need

2 white stones or beads for the centre of the roses
White chalk seed beads or satin beads
Apricot seed beads
Gold seed beads
Gold chunky beads
Size 2 gold bugle beads
Size 3 green bugle beads
Green seed beads
Green cup sequins
Apricot iridescent cup sequins

Method

1. Trace design onto fabric.
2. Sew the stone or bead in the centre of the rose using white thread.
   Thread 1 gold bugle bead and 1 white bead together and sew them beside the centre stone. Insert the needle back into the bugle bead, leaving the white seed bead to anchor on top. Continue in this way until you have two rows of beads standing up around the centre stone.
3. Sew white beads around the edge of the rose, one at a time, moving from right to left.

Bring the two parts of the design together at the dotted lines

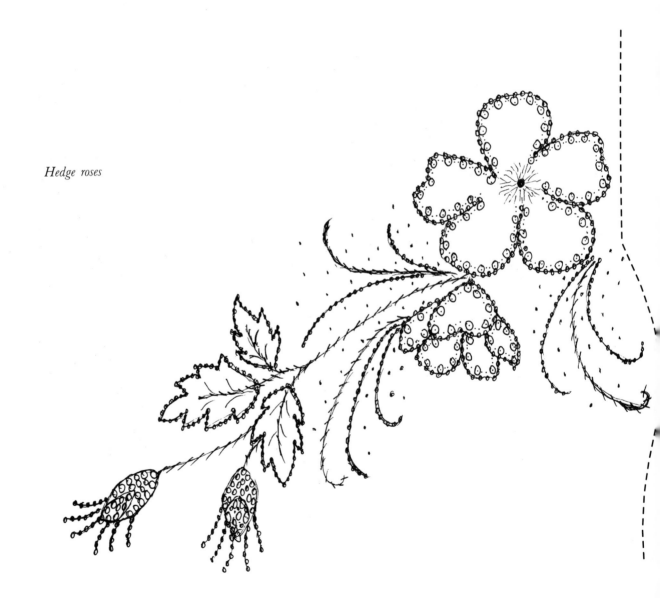

Hedge roses

Inside the line of white beads, using apricot thread, thread 3 apricot seed beads and 1 apricot cup sequin and sew together all around inside the petals. Work both roses and the half bud.

4. Bead the stems with size 3 green bugle beads sewn with a back stitch (see p.13 of *How to Bead*). The stems are continued on into the leaves. Outline the leaves with a single line of green seed beads sewn one at a time.

5. The base of the small buds is worked with green thread and green cup sequins, sewn one at a time. The closed petals are beaded with apricot seed beads and sequins, as worked on the open flowers.

(See sketch.) The slight swirl effect at the point of the buds is beaded flat with green seed beads.

6. The 4 sets of swirls angling out from the roses are worked with size 2 gold bugle beads, seed beads and chunky beads. Use back stitches to sew bugle heads on one swirl in each group. For the other 2 swirls, thread 3 beads together and sew with a whip stitch from right to left.

Spot with single gold chunky beads to finish the design. Mark the spots with a pencil and sew each chunky bead on from spot to spot, ensuring that the fabric does not pucker.

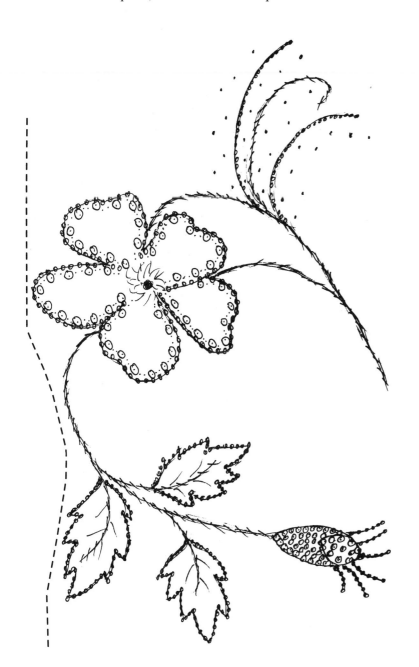

Lace flowers
Plate 10

You will need

Size 1 white satin bugle beads
Size 3 white satin bugle beads
White-lined 3-cut crystal seed beads
Mother of pearl iridescent cup sequins
A small quantity of large white beads
3 white cabochons for the centre of the flowers
Black seed beads for the centres
3 white lace flowers

Method

1. Appliqué lace flowers in position. Trace the scroll design out from the lace flowers.
2. Sew a cabochon onto the centre of each flower. Outline with 7 black seed beads threaded together in a looped fashion so as to stand up around the stone. Repeat once.
3. Work around the appliquéed edge of the flowers with 3 seed beads and 1 sequin threaded together and sewn outwards.
4. Work the main stem of the large scroll with size 1 white bugle beads, sewn individually with a whip stitch from right to left towards yourself. Bead alongside this line with 3 seed beads threaded together and sewn away from yourself. (See sketch.)

5. Work the small leaf shapes with 3 crystal seed beads threaded together and sewn around a single line. Inside each leaf, thread together 3 seed beads, 1 sequin, 1 bead, 1 sequin, 1 bead, 1 sequin and sew from the stem outwards. (See sketch.)

6. For the 7 small swirls on the inside curve of the scrolls, use size 1 bugle beads, sewn individually towards yourself. Between each swirl, sew size 3 white bugle beads, angling outwards. At the top end of the scroll add a large white bead between each bugle bead. Work the second scroll in the same manner.
7. The two single swirls added as a stem effect to one of the lace flowers are worked with size 1 bugle beads.
8. The three additional scrolls around the design are beaded in the same manner as the main stems. Add size 3 bugle beads along the outside edge, angling outwards, with a large white bead in each space. Add spotting of both 3 seed beads and 3 large beads.

Lace flowers

Appliquéed pansies

Plate 11

Open-faced padded pansies make a delightful spray with rouleau stems couched with seed beads and beaded swirls, highlighted with a scattered spotting of cross-cut beads.

You will need

Silk or satin for two pansies and contrasting silk for the stems
Iron-on padding
Seed beads (gun metal with matching bugle beads and sequins have been used here)
Cup sequins
Cross-cut beads for spotting
Size 2 bugle beads for stems and trimmings
Black cup sequins for centre of pansies
An assortment of black cut beads and drops for the hanging arrangements at the centre of the pansies.

Method

1. Make a template of the pansy flower and trace onto contrasting silk, which is then tacked onto iron-on padding. Arrange the pansies onto a blouse or sweater. (See sketch.) Press with a warm iron to hold the padding. Run a tacking thread around the trace marks of the flowers, taking it right through to the fabric. Appliqué around the tacking thread carefully with a machine using a fine zigzag. Trim around close to the machine stitching.
2. Machine stitch the stamens inside the flower also, again using a fine zigzag stitch, as the beading will cover up all of this stitching.
3. Thread 3 seed beads and sew together on the stitched stamens inside the pansies.
4. Bead the outside edge of the flowers. Thread together 3 seed beads, 1 cup sequin, 1 bead, 1 sequin and sew outwards over the raw edge. Continue all around the flowers, shaping carefully.
5. With a pencil mark lines inside each petal to make a fan design, spraying out from the centre. Work size 2 bugle beads with a running stitch along these lines, leaving a tiny space between each bead.
6. For the stems fold a strip of the contrasting silk on the bias. One stem is 25 cm long and the other 44 cm. Machine stitch a tube 1 cm wide, leaving 1 cm for turning, and pull one end through so the fabric is right side out. Thread 2 strands of soft wool through the rouleau for padding. Measure each length of stem and turn the ends in, handstitching neatly.

   Arrange the stems as shown in the design. Stitch to the garment from the wrong side by hand, making sure the stitching is invisible from the right side.

   Couch with 9 seed beads threaded together and spaced evenly down the stem. Press gently on a towel with a warm iron.
7. Trace the swirls as shown in the design. Thread 3 beads together and sew with a whip stitch from right to left, sewing *towards* yourself. Thread size 2 bugle beads and sew with a whip stitch from right to left, *away* from yourself.
8. Sew 1 cross-cut bead at each marked spot.
9. For the centre of the pansies, use large black sequins and chunky black beads. Thread together 2 black beads, 1 sequin, 1 bead, 1 sequin and sew outwards 3 times to give a half-flower shape. Hang the drop arrangement from this centre. (See sketch.)

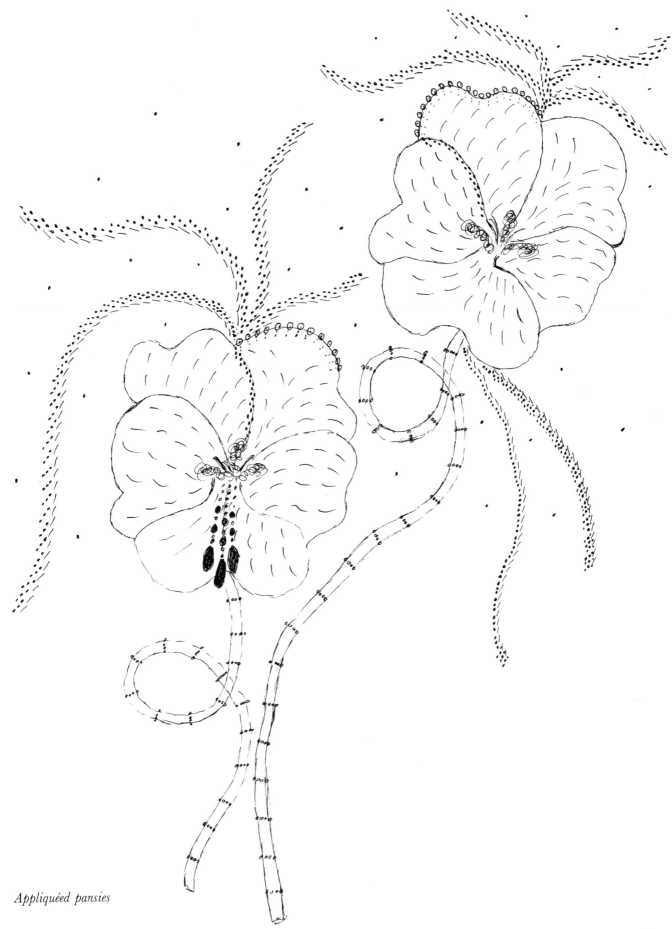

Appliquéed pansies

Native flowers

This combination of wattle, gum blossom and flannel flowers makes an ideal gift and is very inexpensive to work. Instructions for all these flowers are given in *How To Bead*.

You will need

1 oval stretch picture frame (27 × 22 cm)
Fabric (gold furnishing silk illustrated; black would be very striking)

Wattle

Green size 3 bugle beads (for the stems)
Green chunky beads (for the short stalks)
Buttercup-coloured cup sequins, matching beads and thread

Gum blossom

Green size 3 bugle beads (for the stems)
Seed beads
Matching green cup sequins (for the leaves)
A few gold chunky beds
Bronze cup sequins (for base of flower and buds)
Iridescent size 3 bugle beads
Red and green chunky beads (for the flower and buds)

Flannel flower

Green size 3 bugle beads (for the stems)
Tiny green seed beads (for leaves and petal tips)
White crystal or satin beads
Mother of pearl cup sequins
Size 2 light green bugle beads (for the veins of the petals)
Pale green cup sequins and pearls (for the centre of the flower)

Method

1. Dismantle the outer edge of the frame. The fabric is then cut to a larger size than the backing piece.
2. Place interfacing on the wrong side of the fabric; iron-on interfacing is suitable.
3. Lay the fabric on the backing piece of the frame and, with the frame back together, stretch it very taut over the outer edge. Keep moving from side to side and top to bottom making sure the grains of the fabric are left straight.
4. With a marking pencil trace the design carefully, keeping the fabric as taut as possible.
5. After the beading is completed, trim excess fabric away leaving 1 cm to glue down around the back of the frame. Hobby glue is suitable for this. Glue down a length of 1.5 cm wide braid all around to cover up the raw edge of the fabric.

32

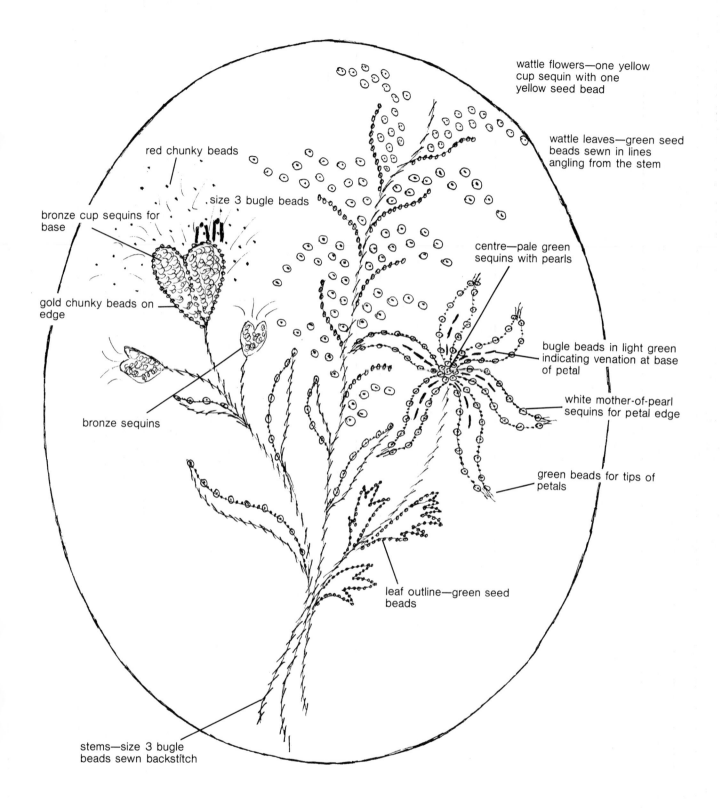

wattle flowers—one yellow
cup sequin with one
yellow seed bead

wattle leaves—green seed
beads sewn in lines
angling from the stem

red chunky beads

size 3 bugle beads

bronze cup sequins for
base

centre—pale green
sequins with pearls

gold chunky beads on
edge

bugle beads in light green
indicating venation at base
of petal

white mother-of-pearl
sequins for petal edge

bronze sequins

green beads for tips of
petals

leaf outline—green seed
beads

stems—size 3 bugle
beads sewn backstitch

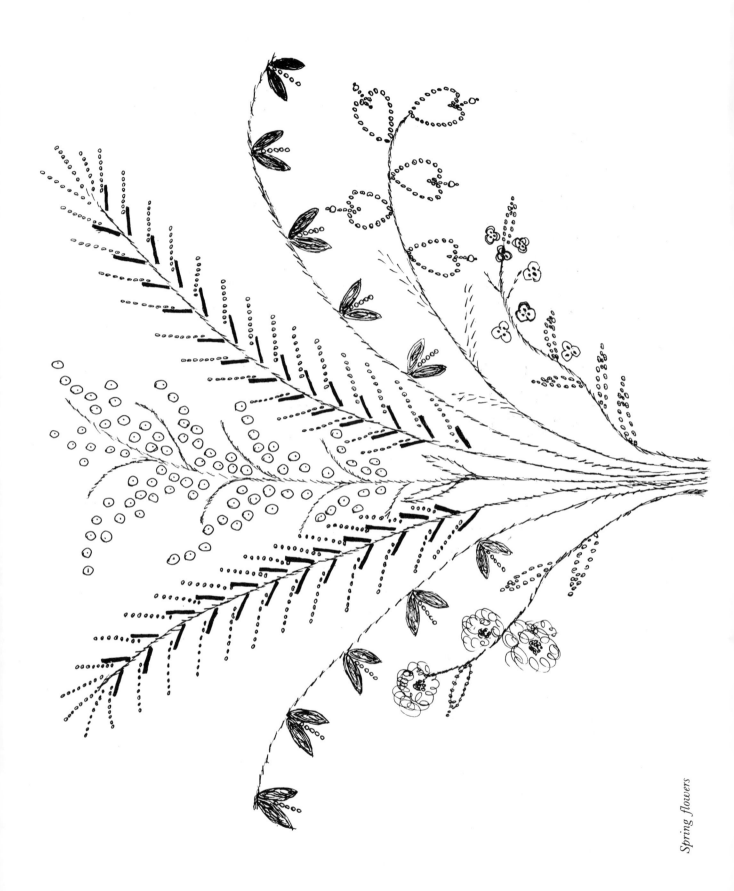

Spring flowers

Spring flowers Plate 13

This spray can be worked on a garment or made into a hanging picture.

You will need

Gold size 1 bugle beads
Gold size 3 bugle beads
Gold seed beads
Green size 1 bugle beads
Green size 2 bugle beads
Oval wooden beads
White chalk beads
A few black seed beads
Buttercup-coloured cup sequins, matching seed beads and thread (for the wattle)
Apricot cup sequins and matching seed beads
Pale blue seed beads (for bluebells)
5 chunky beads (for the end of the hanging stamens)
Darker blue chalk beads (for the forget-me-nots)
Yellow beads (for the centres of the forget-me-nots)

Method

Wattle

1. In the centre of the spray (see sketch), mark the main stem of the wattle sprig and the outward stalks.

   Work the stems with green size 1 bugle beads, sewn individually with a whip stitch from right to left.

2. Mark the individual wattle flowers with dots as a guide. Thread together 1 yellow sequin, from the wrong side, and 1 yellow seed bead. Insert the needle back into the sequin, cup side up. This anchors the bead and sequin.

Wheat

3. Mark a curved line each side of the wattle for the wheat stems. Work with size 1 gold bugle beads sewn individually.

4. Sew size 3 gold bugle beads at an angle outwards from the stem, about 1 cm apart. Work both sides of the stem.

5. Thread 8 tiny gold seed beads together and sew these from just inside the tip of the bugle beads outwards. Work both sides (see sketch). Work a second spray of wheat in the same manner.

Barley grass

6. Mark a curved line to the outside of each stem of barley grass. Work with green size 2 bugle beads sewn individually.

   From the end of the curve sew 2 oval wooden beads in a V fashion, angling downwards. Thread together 5 white chalk beads and sew these in the centre of the V. Work 5 flowers along each stem, spaced about 3.5 cm apart.

Black-eyed Susan

7. On the left side of the spray, mark a curved line to take the 3 small flowers. Work the stem with green size 1 bugle beads. Mark a dot where each flower is to go. For the centre of the flower, thread 3 black seed beads together and sew in a cluster. Repeat this twice.

8. Thread together 3 apricot seed beads and 1 apricot cup sequin, and work around the centre 8 times to fashion the flower.

9. Mark 3 small straight lines for the split leaves (follow the sketch). Thread 6 green beads together and sew outwards from the stem, anchoring with a small stitch. Thread a further 6 beads, bring these back to the stem and take another small stitch. Pass the needle halfway beween these two lines. Thread together a further 4 beads and sew them in the middle of the leaf point, forming a split leaf. Repeat to make 3 leaves from the stem.

Bluebells

10. On the right draw another curved stem for the bluebells, working it with green beads in the same manner as the others. Mark 1 bluebell at the end of the stem, then 2 more to each side. Work blue seed beads individually around the marked shape of the bells. From the centre of each bell, thread 3 seed beads, 1 larger bead, 1 seed bead and insert the needle back, leaving the seed bead to anchor the hanging stamen.

Forget-me-nots

11. On the right mark a final curved stem for the forget-me-nots, and work it with green beads. Mark 7 dots to represent the flowers, and sew 3 yellow seed beads in a cluster for the centres.

12. To make this tiny flower, thread together 5 blue beads and sew these outside each cluster of yellow beads in a looped fashion 3 times.

13. Add 5 split leaves down the stem. (See sketch.)

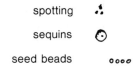

spotting

sequins

seed beads

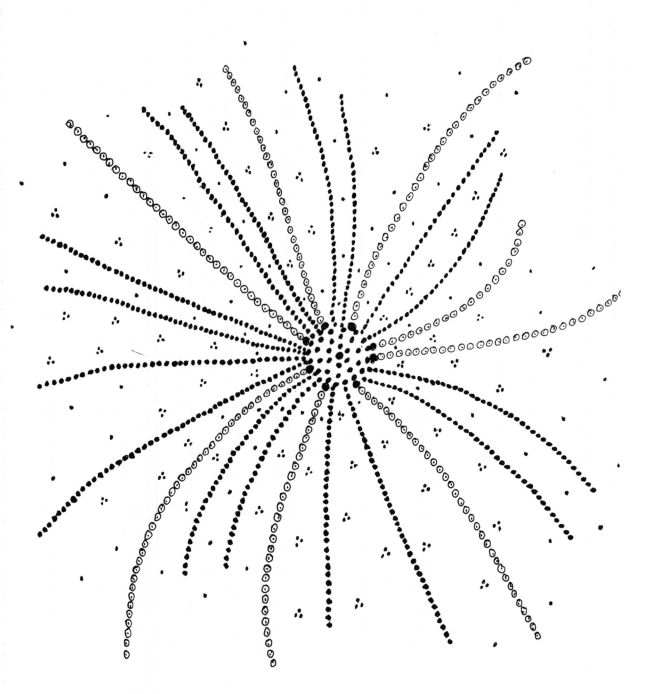

Sunburst—instructions for this design appear on page 41

Plate 9 Wisteria *(page 24)*

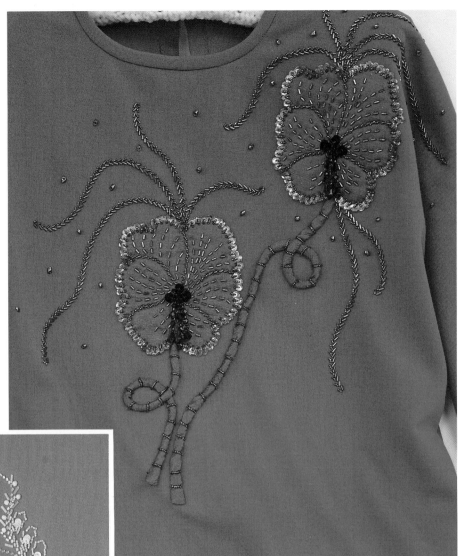

Plate 11 Sweater worked with beaded appliquéed pansies (page 30)

Plate 10 Beaded appliquéed lace flowers (page 28)

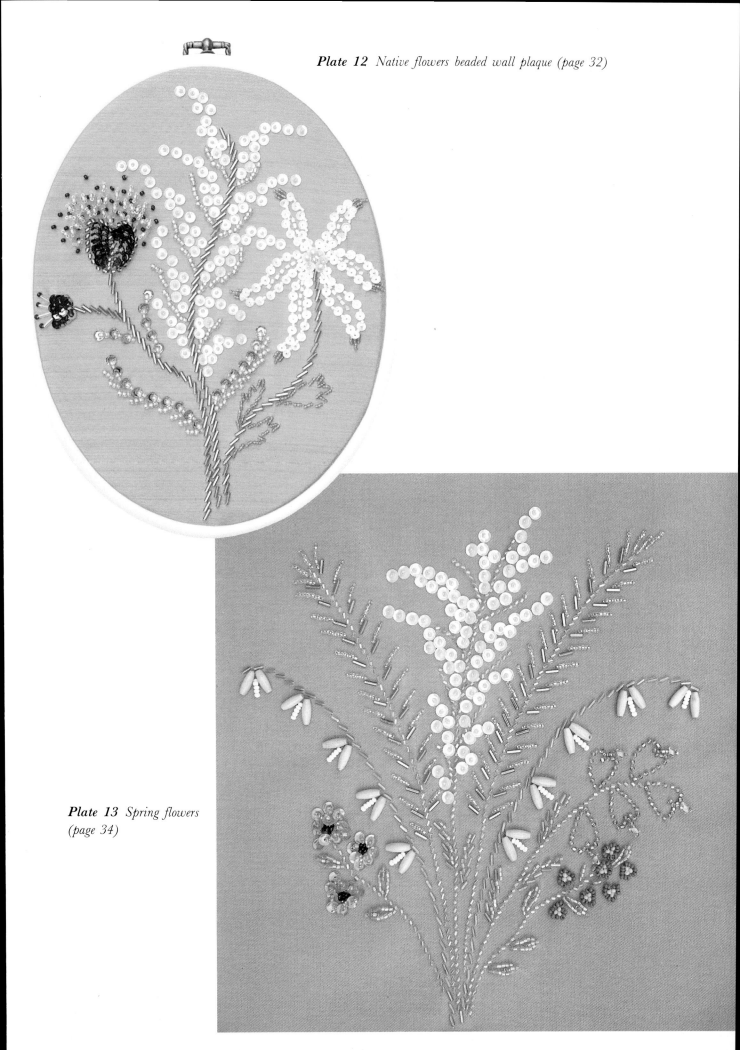

Plate 12 *Native flowers beaded wall plaque (page 32)*

Plate 13 *Spring flowers (page 34)*

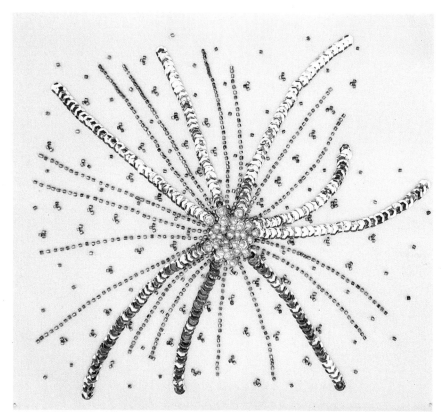

Plate 14 Sunburst motif *(page 36)*

Plate 15 Wattle spray *(page 41)*

Sunburst
Plate 14

The design appears on page 36.

Tambour or hand beading can be used for this very simple design consisting of slightly curved lines flowing from the centre to different lengths and spaced at varying intervals.

You will need

Bronze cut seed beads
Bronze cup sequins
Cream seed pearls for the centre

Method

1. The beads and sequins are all worked one at a time.
2. The centre section is worked with cup sequins surmounted by pearls. Thread a sequin from the wrong side, then a pearl, and insert the needle back through the sequin to anchor. Start from the very centre and bead around it with 28 sequins and pearls.
3. The cluster spotting consists of 3 beads sewn on separately, graduating to 2 beads and finally 1 bead.

Wattle
Plate 15

The wattle spray has stems of green bugle beads with flowers formed of yellow sequins with a seed bead in the middle of each.

You will need

Buttercup-coloured cup sequins
Matching seed beads and thread
Size 1 green bugle beads
Size 2 green bugle beads

Method

This sketch illustrates just one part of the wattle spray in Plate 15. You may like to make your own design based on this sketch.

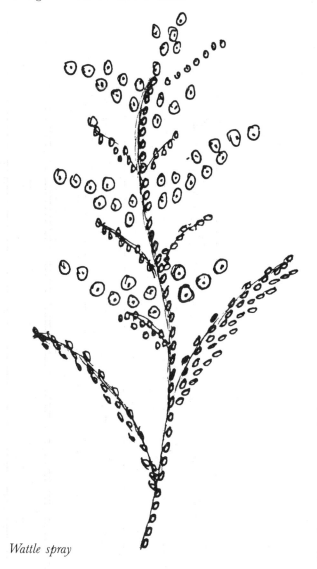

Wattle spray

Beaded lace butterflies

Beaded lace butterflies

Plate 16

You will need

Lace butterflies (these can be obtained from department stores or craft shops)
Black seed beads
2 small black cup sequins
2 tiny rosemonties for the eyes
2 larger rosemonties for the wings
Jade iridescent chunky beads
Jade iridescent crystal cup sequins
Clear iridescent cup sequins
Size 2 green bugle beads
Green seed beads
2 shades of pink seed beads
Lemon seed beads
Blue seed beads

Method

1. Cut around the edge of the lace butterfly and arrange onto a blouse or jacket (as in design). Appliqué lace onto fabric by machine or by hand.
2. Sew the two tiny rosemonties above the body for the eyes. Work black seed beads from the eyes for the antennae, ending with a small black cup sequin, cup side up, anchored with a black seed bead in its centre.
3. Starting at the head, bead the body crosswise with black seed beads. Start with 2 beads together on the needle and repeat. Increase to 3 beads and then 5, shaping the body. Graduate the beads down the body to 1 bead (work 5 single beads).
4. Sew the larger rosemonties onto the lower wings (see sketch). Using jade beads sew around the edge of the stone, then sew another 3 beads in a line from the stone to the body.
5. Using jade chunky beads, sew 1 bead at a time around the edge of the butterfly, with a whip stitch from right to left.
6. Thread 2 jade beads and 1 jade sequin together and sew these inside the tiny scallops on the large part of the wings. Fill part of the top wings with 3 rows of alternating jade and crystal iridescent cup sequins.
7. With a marking pencil trace the swirls for the stems of the flowers (see sketch). Work with pale green seed beads threaded together in 3s and sewn down with a whip stitch, from right to left.
8. Mark 3 dots and sew a black seed bead onto each for the centre of the daisies. (See sketch.)
9. Mark 6 lines for the petals. Thread together 5 pale pink beads and sew from the centre outwards, flat onto the fabric. Thread together 3 darker pink beads and sew between each of the first 6 petals. This gives an attractive variegated look.
10. For the centres of the forget-me-nots, mark 3 dots and sew 3 lemon seed beads onto each.
    Thread 5 blue seed beads together and sew around the lemon beads three times in a looped fashion.
11. Work size 2 green bugle beads individually, at an angle, down both sides of the outside swirl. Scatter some small Vs around the flowers using green bugle beads.

dangling arrangements

Octopus scroll motif

44

Octopus scroll motif

Plate 18

This design looks very complicated but is actually quite simple to bead. The wooden beads in dark brown and natural shades and the shot bronze beads are highlighted with black beads and sequins.

You will need

Size 2 shot bronze bugle beads
Shot bronze seed beads
Gold chunky beads
Bronze cup sequins
Black chunky beads
Large black sequins with a hole on the edge
Tiny silver metal seed beads
Cream seed pearls

For the centre flower and dangling arrangements

2 large wooden beads
1 oval wooden bead
5 wooden beads
8 small wooden beads
5 oval cut black beads
5 small black cut beads
Black cup sequins
Gold chunky beads
Black chunky beads

Method

There are altogether 14 scroll lines with 4 different bead patterns; 3 of these are executed 4 times, and the fourth twice only.

Scroll 1

1. Sew size 2 shot bronze bugle beads individually along the line using whip stitches, from right to left, leaving a small space between each bead.
2. Thread together 3 bronze seed beads and sew across the line in each space between the bugle beads.

   Repeat this row 3 more times on the design. (See sketch.)

Scroll 2

1. Work gold chunky beads and dark brown oval wooden beads alternately along the line with a whip stitch.

2. Working outwards from a chunky bead, thread a further 2 chunky beds, 1 cup sequin, 1 bead, 1 large black sequin. Sew this combination on alternate sides of every third chunky bead.

   Repeat this row 3 more times on the design. (See sketch.)

Scroll 3

This scroll is a combination of natural small round wooden beads, gold chunky beads, bronze sequins, black chunky beads and tiny silver metal seed beads.

1. Working towards yourself, moving from right to left with whip stitches, thread together 2 bronze chunky beads, 1 sequin, then 1 round wooden bead and sew along the line, finishing with the bronze beads and sequin on the end.
2. Mark small swirls along this scroll, alternately to each side. Bead each swirl with black chunky beads sewn individually. On the inside curves of the swirls, work groups of 3 silver beads threaded together and sewn close to the black beads. Add 1 seed pearl and 3 spots of 1 single silver bead. (See sketch.)

   Repeat this row 3 more times on the design.

Scroll 4

Work this line with bronze chunky beads, sewn individually. Repeat the line once.

Half flower at the centre of the design

Using black chunky beads and the larger size black cup sequins, thread together 3 beads, 1 sequin, 1 bead, 1 sequin, 1 bead, 1 sequin, 1 bead, 1 sequin, and sew outwards from the centre point of the motif. Repeat this twice to each side of the first line and once again to each side, omitting 1 bead and 1 sequin. Sew dangling arrangements from this half flower.

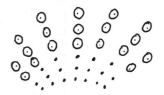

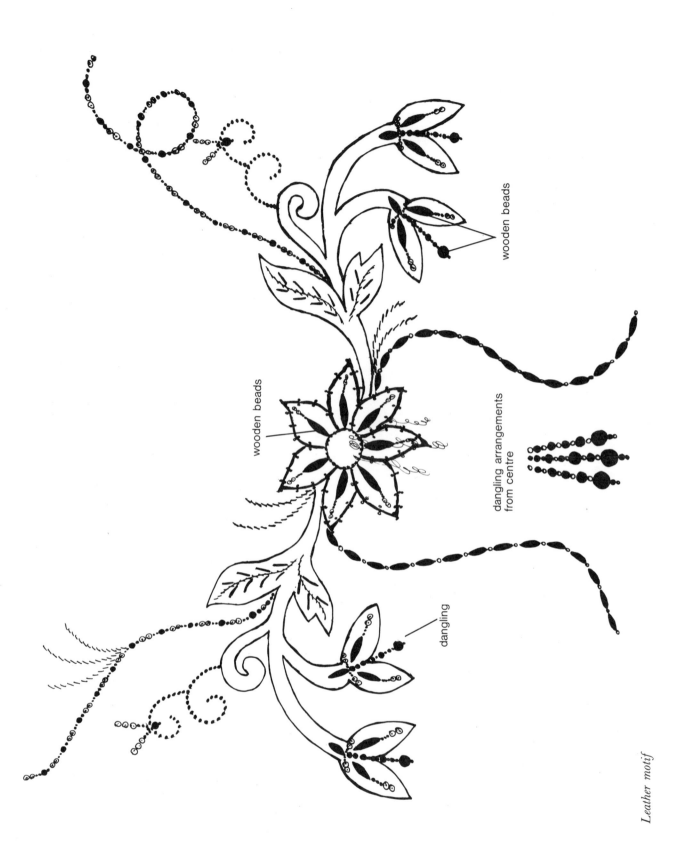

wooden beads

wooden beads

dangling arrangements from centre

dangling

Leather motif

46

Leather motif

This embroidered leather design uses brown and natural shades of wooden beads, bronze beads and sequins. Leather colours other than tan could be used, but it might be necessary to change the colours of the beads.

You will need

Pieces of tan-coloured feather leather
Dark brown oval wooden beads
Natural shades of oval and small wooden beads
Bronze chunky beads
Size 3 bronze bugle beads
Size 2 bronze bugle beads
Size 1 bronze bugle beads
Bronze seed beads
Bronze cup sequins

For the dangling arrangements

3 large round natural wooden beads
15 smaller round natural wooden beads

Some craft shops sell scraps of leather which are very suitable for bead work, but they must be washed to remove any dye. Wash in warm water with a little hair shampoo and keep washing and rinsing until the water is clear. Roll onto a towel, smooth out and lay flat in the shade to dry. The feather leather used here is soft and easy to work with.

Method

1. First trace the motif onto the leather with a marking pencil and cut around it carefully. Arrange the design across the front of a blouse or sweater, placing the large starflower in the centre, then pin carefully around the edge.
2. With a single strand of matching machine thread, sew a tiny hemming stitch by hand all around the edge of the flower. (This will hold your work in place for machine stitching.)
   Carefully appliqué all around the flower with a sewing machine, using a tiny close zigzag stitch.
   Do not use satin appliqué stitch. A little patience will be needed. Place the remainder of the design in position as shown in the sketch. Pin, hand sew and machine stitch in the same

manner as for the centre flower. Press on the wrong side with a warm iron.
3. Using matching double thread, work size 2 bronze bugle beads individually around the edge of the starflower. Thread together 3 bronze seed beads and sew across between each bugle bead. This will highlight the flower.
4. On each petal of the flower work 1 natural oval wooden bead, sewing out from the centre. Continuing from the wooden bead, thread together 3 bronze seed beads, 1 bronze sequin, 1 bead, 1 sequin and sew.
5. Work the leaf veins with size 2 bronze bugle beads, using a back stitch. To each side of these lines, sew size 3 bronze bugle beads angling outwards.
6. Work the two scrolls trailing downwards from the flower with single dark brown oval wooden beads alternated with bronze chunky beads. Sew with a whip stitch from right to left.
7. The four small scrolls marked from the leaf tendrils are worked with bronze chunky beads, sewn individually.
   From the second scroll on each side projects a V of beads and sequins threaded together. In the centre of the V thread together 2 seed beads, 1 round natural wooden bead, 1 chunky bead, and insert the needle back through the beads leaving the end bead to anchor. This will dangle.

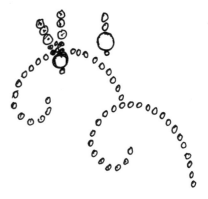

8. The two swirls emerging from the centre flower are worked with size 1 bronze bugle beads, sewn from right to left with a whip stich.
9. For the two heavier beaded scrolls trailing outwards above the leaves to both sides you will need small round wooden beads, bronze chunky beads, bronze seed beads and sequins.
   From the edge of the lefthand leather leaf, thread together 2 bronze seed beads, 1 sequin, 1 bead, 1 sequin and sew from right to left with

a whip stitch, working towards yourself. Work 1 round wooden bead, then 1 bronze chunky bead. Continue in this manner to the end of the line. Work 3 swirls outwards from the sixth wooden bead with size 1 bronze bugle beads sewn individually. (See sketch.)

Work the scroll on the right in the same manner, omitting the swirls.

10. For the details on the leather buds, sew 1 natural oval wooden bead on each petal. From the lower end of each bud, thread together 3 bronze seed beads, 1 sequin, 1 bead, 1 sequin and sew down (as on the centre flower petals). Between the two oval wooden beads sew 3 small round wooden beads. Bring the needle back to the last wooden bead and thread 3 bronze seed beads, 1 small round wooden bead, 3 seed beads, 1 large round wooden bead, 1 bronze bead. Insert the needle back through the beads leaving the bronze bead to anchor. This forms a dangling stamen.

Above the top round wooden bead, sew 1 dark brown wooden bead, and on each side thread 3 bronze seed beads, 1 sequin, 1 bead, 1 sequin and sew these outwards.

11. To complete the beading, sew the dangling arrangements from the centre of the flower, referring to the sketch for the number of beads on each string.

Plate 16
*Beaded lace
butterflies
(page 42)*

Plate 17 *Haircombs decorated with sequin
flowers (page 54)*

Plate 18
*Octopus scroll
motif worked
on a pullover
(page 44)*

Plate 19
*Beaded leather
design worked
on a sweater
(page 46)*

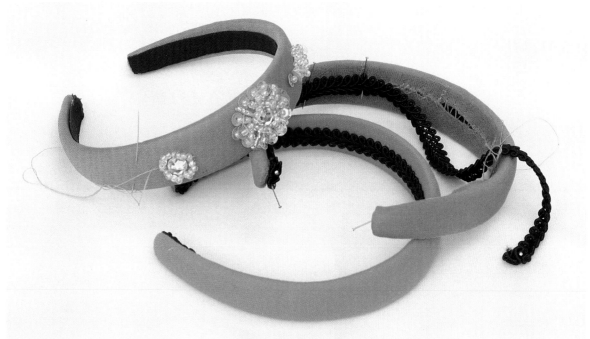

Plate 20 Beading a headband
(page 54)

Plate 21 Beaded headbands
(page 54)

Plate 22 *1920s georgette blouse beaded with a crazy design (page 58)*

Hair accessories

Sequin flowers

Plate 17

These sequinned flowers make ideal gifts for all ages.

You will need

A bead needle
Large pearl or bead for the centre of the flower
Sequins (large or small with a hole on the side) for the flowers (colours to suit)
Chunky beads (to match the sequins)
Any scrap of silk material
A small amount of buckram (approx. 30 cm)
A packet of long bobby pins

Method

1. Cut 2 pieces of stiffening, about the size of a 20 cent coin, then 2 pieces of silk the same size (the colour of both to match the sequins used). Place the 2 pieces of stiffening between the two pieces of silk and thread them onto one arm of a bobby pin through the centre of the fabrics. Holding the bobby pin in place, buttonhole firmly around the raw edges.
2. On the right side, using a double polyester thread secured with a knot, make a small stitch in the centre of the circle and thread the large centre bead and 1 chunky bead. Insert the needle back through the large bead to the wrong side leaving the chunky bead to anchor it. Sew another small stitch on the wrong side to hold the large bead firm.
3. Insert the needle back to the right side, next to the large bead. Thread 9 chunky beads together and sew these in a loop fashion 4 times so they stand up around the large bead.
   Note: Be careful not to take any thread over the bobby pin on the wrong side. Keep this free or it will not be able to slide over the hair.
4. Insert your needle and thread back to the right side, close to the looped beads. Thread together 1 sequin, 1 bead, 1 sequin, 1 bead, 1 sequin and pull these into place so that the first sequin stands up against the large bead and the last sequin lays flat around the edge. Repeat this 14 times around the large bead to form the flower, making sure the thread does not tangle.

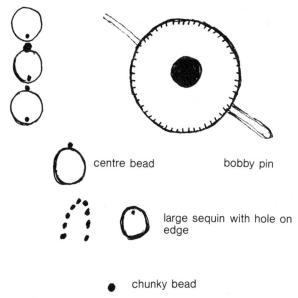

centre bead   bobby pin

large sequin with hole on edge

chunky bead

Sequin flower

Combs with sequin flowers Plate 17

These combs can be made in all colours and make lovely gifts.

You will need

1 comb, any size
5 cm wide ribbon to match sequins and chunky beads
3 large pearls or beads for the centres of the flowers

Method

Hold the ribbon firm against the right side of the comb. Wind the ribbon firmly between the teeth of the comb, keeping it as flat as possible, then sew the flowers in the same manner as for the bobby pin flower (p. 53), omitting the looped beads around the large centre bead. The flowers will be a little smaller as there is very little space on the top of the comb to sew into. Small combs will hold 3 flowers and larger combs 4 flowers.

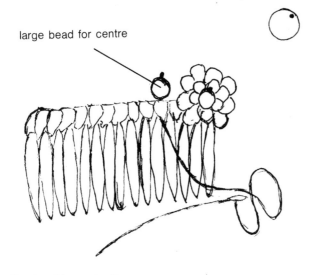

large bead for centre

Comb with sequin flowers

Jewelled headbands Plate 20, 21

These jewelled headbands make an elegant headdress for a bride and bridesmaids.

You will need

Plastic headband (these headbands can be purchased quite cheaply already covered, and the covering removed). Fabric, silk or jersey is suitable.
Soft padding, iron-on is suitable
Braid for inside the band
Assortment of gold, silver and iridescent beads and cup sequins, size 3 bugle beads, rhinestones, crystal rosemonties and large and small pearls, as desired, to match covering fabric

Method

1. Cover the plastic band with 2 layers of iron-on padding (or any soft padding). Press with a warm iron to hold. Trim away the padding to the edge of the plastic.
2. Cut a strip of fabric on the bias, enough to fit over the padded band and be sewn together on the inside. Allow for a decrease in width as the material is stretched firmly.
3. Using doubled machine thread, sew the covering fabric together inside the band, catching each edge with a good-sized top stitch, and pulling the fabric taut. Turn the end edges over and sew neatly. Make sure the fabric over the band is stretched taut.
4. Cut a length of 1.5 cm wide braid, fold one end under and stitch to the fabric at one end on the inside of the band. Use hobby glue to fasten the braid down over the seam in the fabric. Secure the braid with a few stitches at the other end. Leave until the glue is dry before starting to embroider. Be careful not to get glue on the padding—when dry it sets hard and is impossible to sew through.

Embroidering the band

Beginners should initially bead something simple, then progress to more elaborate motifs.
1. Measure the length of the band and mark the centre with a marking pencil.
    For sewing beads and sequins to the headband the needle and thread must be passed from side to side as it is not possible to sew directly through.

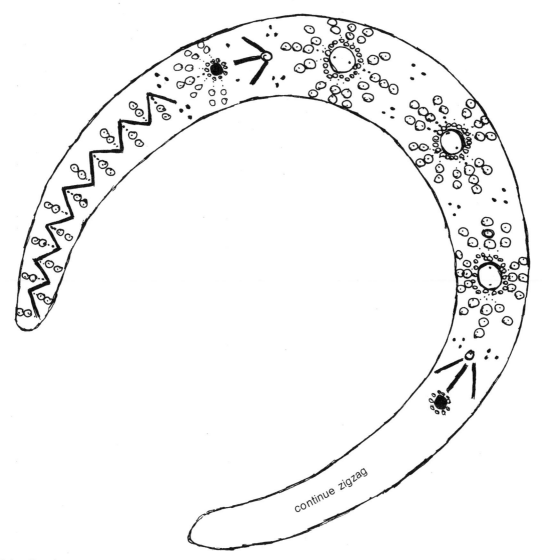

Jewelled headband

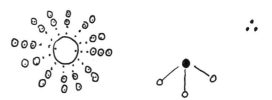

Anchor the doubled matching thread on the centre mark.

2. Start by sewing a sequin flower with a small silver rhinestone or pearl for the centre.

   Hold the rhinestone in the centre and sew into each hole. Thread together 5 chunky beads and sew these in a looped fashion around the stone.

   Thread 2 chunky beads, 1 iridescent cup sequin, 1 bead, 1 sequin, 1 bead, 1 sequin and slide the needle across to the opposite side of the stone and repeat. Repeat all around omitting 1 bead and 1 sequin. (See sketch.)

   Work another flower each side of the centre one, to give 3 flowers, spaced 4.5 cm apart.

3. Working away from the centre, sew 3 bugle beads from 1 pearl, then some cluster spotting of 3 beads. Next, sew a rosemontie with a half flower. From here, work zigzag fashion to the end of the band. (The zigzag method is explained in *How To Bead*, p.38.)

4. Work the second side to match the first.

If necessary, a comb can be sewn in to hold the band in place

55

Small headband

Plate 21

Children love to have something special to wear to parties and this is ideal for such an occasion.

Very narrow plastic headbands 1 cm wide are available, and these are suitable for a child. These bands are easy to cover.

1. Cut a strip of material on the bias, the length of the band and wide enough to cover both sides with a seam.
2. Stitch on the machine, making a rouleau 1 cm wide, then pull through right side out. Thread this onto the plastic band and stretch firm. Turn the ends inside and stitch neatly.
3. Mark the centre and sew a few rosemontie beads and sequins for glitter.

Tambour or French frame beading

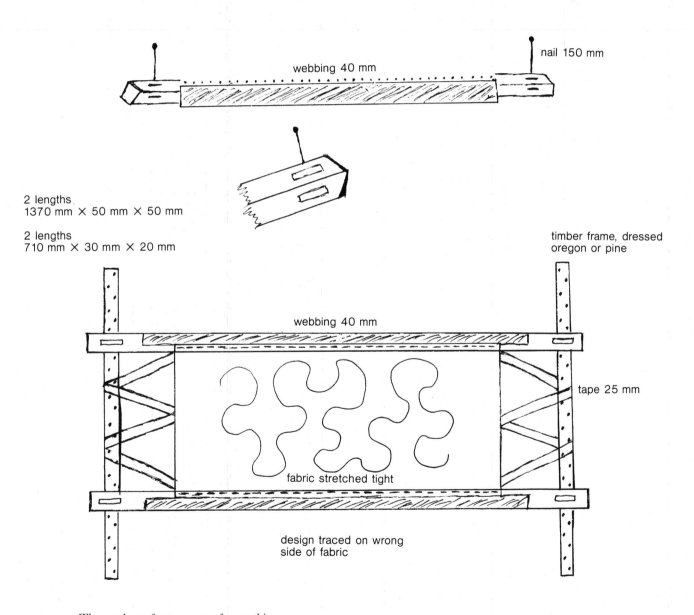

nail 150 mm

webbing 40 mm

2 lengths
1370 mm × 50 mm × 50 mm

2 lengths
710 mm × 30 mm × 20 mm

timber frame, dressed
oregon or pine

webbing 40 mm

tape 25 mm

fabric stretched tight

design traced on wrong
side of fabric

The tambour frame set up for working

1920s georgette blouse

Plate 22

This blouse has a loose fitting elbow-length magyar sleeve and a slightly dropped waistline, finished with a tie band draped to one side and ending in a single looped fringe of beads.

You will need

1.3 m of 115 cm georgette or sheer crepe fabric
Crystal cut seed beads
Matching thread

Method

1. Cut a pattern to your measurements. Lay the pattern onto fabric and trace all around the neck, sleeve, side seams, etc., with a tacking thread. *Do not cut out.*

   Pin all the fabric to each side of the webbing on the tambour frame, then stitch with some strong thread, using long tacking stitches. As you will have quite a lot of fabric to handle, roll part of this on one side of the wood with sheets of tissue paper to protect the fabric. Place the end woods through and anchor the nails, then pull firm and tape each end. *It must be taut.*

2. The blouse is embroidered with an all-over crazy design. If you cannot freehand this design, it can be traced with a marking pencil as you progress. A little patience and practice may be needed. Thread a number of beads onto the spool of thread attached to the nail on the lefthand side of the tambour frame.

3. Using the tambour needleholder, pull the thread through the fabric to the wrong side, and hold to anchor. When starting, with the needle make two tiny chain stitches (thread only). At the end of each section make two small anchor stitches (thread only). You are working on the wrong side of the fabric—the beads are underneath.

   Cover all the garment with the crazy design.

4. To make up the garment, cut all around the marking thread, allowing 1.5 cm for seams.

   Pin all seams together and sew with a fine back stitch. Turn in the seam allowance on the edge of the sleeves and hem neatly. Measure the length of the neck opening and cut a strip of fabric on the bias. Sew by hand to finish the neck edge. A few beads can be added.

   Cut two lengths of fabric 72 cm × 14 cm wide for the tie. Join the two lengths together. Pin this to fit the lower edge of the blouse and sew carefully by machine as you may be close to beads. Sew the two end pieces for the tie, turn and press.

5. With a bead needle, thread 40 seed beads at a time to make a single looped fringe around the edges of the sleeves and tie. Press carefully on a towel with a warm iron.

Crazy design for 1920s georgette blouse

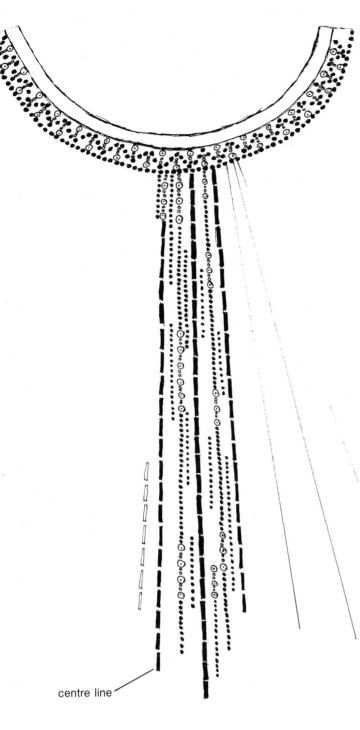

centre line

repeat this section,
spacing the bugle bead
lines in a sunray from the
neckline

Radiating design for black sheer crepe embroidered blouse

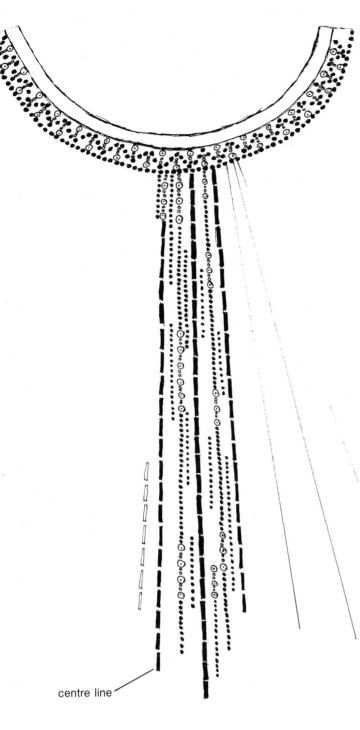

Embroidered blouse

Plate 23

The black sheer crepe blouse is beaded with gunmetal beads and sequins.

You will need

1.30 m of 115 cm wide material
Gunmetal cut seed beads
Gunmetal cup sequins
Size 2 gunmetal bugle beads

Method

The design is made up of broken straight lines radiating from the neck downwards. Every fifth line is interrupted with size 2 bugle beads. In between these lines are broken lines of seed beads.

Hand beading between the breaks with three beads and a sequin gives a sunray effect. All the seams are hand sewn from the shoulder so as not to disturb the beads. The neck facing was sewn on by hand with sequins and beads to finish the neckline.

Georgette chemise blouse

Plate 24

The design consists of a sunray of beads cascading from a jewelled clasp motif embroidered on the left shoulder. A rouleau threaded through the hemline ties with a bow. The swirling lines are very simple to bead: each line is worked with a single type of bead, and the different types are rotated across the lines.

You will need

Georgette, hot pink as illustrated
Chunky and seed beads to match
Size 2 bugle beads

Method

1. Mark onto fabric (to your measurements) an opera-top neckline and armholes. Trace around with a tacking thread. *Do not* cut out, as this has to be beaded on the tambour frame. Only the front of the garment is to be worked.

Plate 23 *Sheer crepe blouse beaded with gunmetal beads and sequins (page 60)*

Plate 24 *Georgette chemise blouse with a beaded sunray radiating from a clasp motif (page 60)*

61

Plate 25 *Detail of beaded hibiscus flower*

Plate 26 *Charleston-look blouse with all-over hibispattern and looped bead fringe (page 66)*

Plate 27 Drawstring evening bag with beaded Indian design (page 70)

Plate 28 A crepe evening gown from 1964 embroidered by the tambour technique, with flowers and hanging drops worked by hand. This gown is adorned with matching sequins, iridescent crystal beads, pale green baroque pearls and hanging crystals

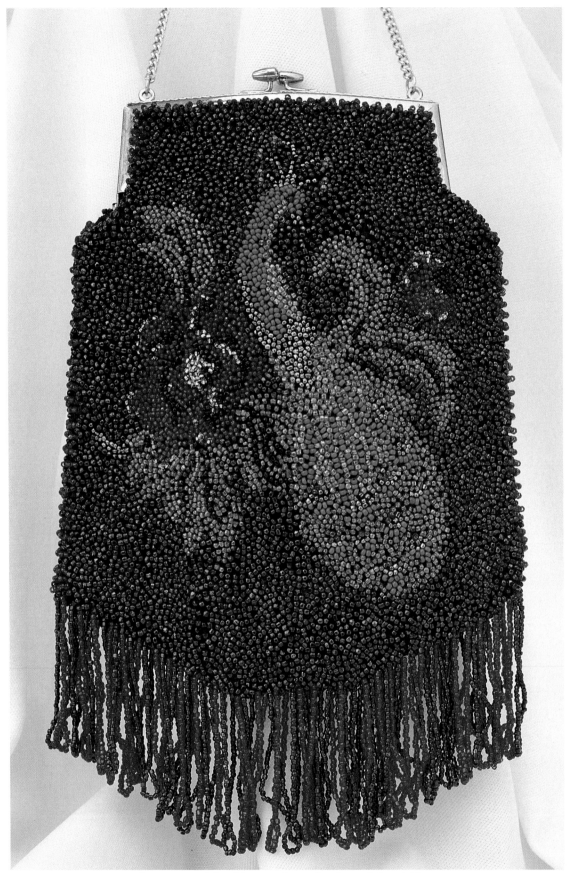

Plate 29 *Tambour beading was used for this peacock evening bag of the 1800s*

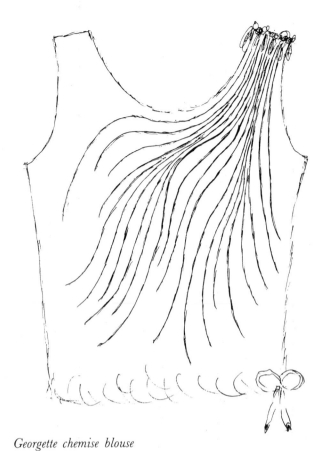

Georgette chemise blouse

2. Tack the fabric onto the webbing at each side with strong thread. Pull out taut, fasten with nails and tape each end to make it all firm.

3. With matching free-running thread anchored onto the nail on your left side, thread a long string of beads. Some beads come in bunches. If so tie a slip knot and pass the beads over the knot onto the thread you are beading with. The other alternative is to thread each bead individually.

4. Using the tambour needle, pull thread through and hold, then make two tiny stitches (thread only) to anchor. Then, moving one bead at a time to the fabric underneath, make a chain stitch for each bead. Continue with this method on all the lines. When you come to the end of a line, anchor in the same way with two tiny stitches (thread only). Work each line in one type of bead, rotating the 3 different types across the lines.

5. When all the beading is complete, remove from the frame. Cut out the garment all around the tacking thread, *leaving a seam allowance.* Then cut out the back and pin all together. The garment can be stitched together by machine. Finish the neck and armhole edges with a length of fabric cut on the bias. Stitch onto garment, trim the seam, then roll and turn, sewing neatly by hand on the inside.

6. Stitch a 3 cm wide hem, leaving an opening on the left side to thread the rouleau through.

7. Cut another length of fabric 152 cm × 8 cm on the bias for the draw string. Stitch this 1.5 cm wide, but *do not trim fabric.* Pull all this through right side out, turn in each end and stitch neatly. Thread the rouleau through the hemline, leaving it long enough to tie a soft bow at the left side. At each end of the rouleau tie a soft knot to finish.

The left shoulder is finished with a jewelled motif stitched to the shoulder line.

Method

1. Cut a piece of buckram or interfacing the size of a 50 cent coin and cover with double fabric.

2. In the centre of the coin shape sew a silver rhinestone surrounded with rosemonties. Work all around the rosemonties with chunky beads.

3. Work around outside the rosemonties with beads and matching cup sequins, and 8 teardrop pearls as in sketch.

4. Work loops of hanging crystal beads around the edge of the motif.

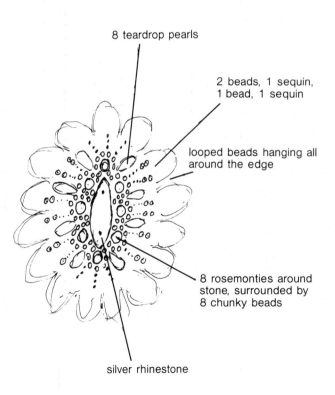

8 teardrop pearls

2 beads, 1 sequin, 1 bead, 1 sequin

looped beads hanging all around the edge

8 rosemonties around stone, surrounded by 8 chunky beads

silver rhinestone

1920s Charleston-look blouse

Plates 25, 26

Tambour beading is used for the hibiscus open-flower design on this georgette blouse. Beaded borders finish the edges of the garment, with a long single-looped fringe on the hem line for shimmer.

You will need

Cream georgette or similar fabric (1 m × 115 cm)
Iridescent crystal cut seed beads
Size 3 iridescent bugle beads
Size 1 iridescent bugle beads
Iridescent mother-of-pearl sequins for a cup flower in the centre of each hibiscus
Small seed pearls for the centre
Matching thread

Method

1. Choose a simple dropped-shoulder pattern with a round neck, cut to your measurements. Lay the front and back patterns onto the fabric, and trace around them with a tacking thread. *Do not cut the blouse out*; leave the fabric all in one piece for attaching to the tambour frame. Tack the front of the blouse onto the frame webbing with a strong thread. Stretch the fabric tight with the nail holders, and then tape the ends.

Neck and armhole borders

2. For the neck border, starting from the top, thread size 3 bugle beads onto free-running machine thread. Holding this thread with the left hand, pull thread through to the wrong side with the tambour needle. Hold and make two tiny chain stitches to anchor (thread only). Moving a bugle bead to the material, make a chain stitch the size of the bugle bead to hold it, and work the bugle beads zigzag fashion. Take a tiny stitch to hold each bugle bead firm.

3. Move 4 crystal beads together, and work these below each bugle bead. Make another small stitch as before to hold beads firm.

4. Mark with pencil 2.25 cm from the neck edge, all around the shape of the neck. Bead size 3 bugle beads on this line, taking a small stitch between each bead.

5. Move 4 seed beads together, beading zigzag fashion over each bugle bead.

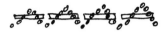

   Mark another line 2.25 cm from the first, and repeat the previous pattern. The neck border is 4.5 cm wide.

6. Work the Cornaly crazy pattern with seed beads between the two rows you have beaded.

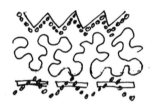

7. Repeat the first section of the neck edge around the armhole border, 2.5 cm.

8. The lower hem line of the blouse above the fringe is worked with the zigzag pattern only.

9. Make a template of the hibiscus flower for tracing the pattern onto the fabric. Leave sufficient space in the centre to embroider a small sequinned cup flower around a small pearl.

10. Thread 46 cm of crystal beads together onto the matching thread on the large spool. Move 3 beads to the fabric together, making a stitch with your tambour needle about 0.5 cm long. Continue in this way all around the edge of the flower. This method produces a picot-edge effect.

This sketch is to a
small scale. Only the
neck border and
template for the
hibiscus flower are
approximately actual
size

1920s Charleston-look blouse

11. Mark 3 lines in a nested V fashion inside each petal. For the first line use crystal seed beads, and for the second line size 3 bugle beads. Make a small stitch between each bugle bead. The third line is worked with size 1 bugle beads. Bead a V with two size 3 bugle beads to highlight the centre of each petal and between each petal. End each section of beading with two very small stitches (thread only).

12. The swirls coming from between the petals can be worked with alternated seed beads and size 1 bugle beads. A spotting of groups of 3 beads and single beads is then scattered all over the blouse.

Finishing

13. For the hem-line fringe, thread together a number of beads (this fringe requires a lot of beads). Mark a 7 cm section on the webbing of your frame so you can measure the beads on the thread for each loop (twice 7 cm). Remember to secure each loop of beads with a tiny stitch (thread only). Continue the loops all around the hem line.

   When the above beading is completed, carefully remove the fabric from the frame.

14. Next, embroider the cup flowers in the centre of each hibiscus. Sew a small pearl in the centre. Then thread together 3 seed beads, 1 sequin, 1 bead, 1 sequin and sew outwards from the pearl. Repeat this eight times to form the small flower.

15. Cut out the blouse, pin, matching the neck and armhole borders. Handstitch all seams neatly with a small back stitch. Trim, then oversew all

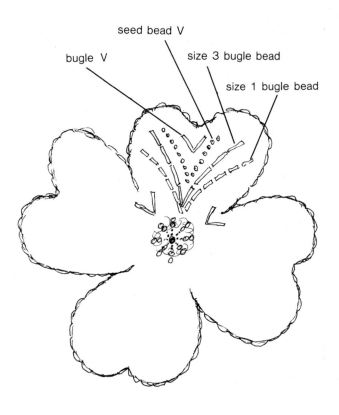

hibiscus open flower

raw edges neatly. Turn up the armhole edges and lower hem line and slip stitch neatly.

   To finish the neck line, cut a strip of fabric on the bias. Sew this by hand with a small back stitch close to the beads. Turn inside and slip stitch neatly. Press gently on a towel with a warm iron.

16. Finally, make a looped edge around the neck and armholes with 7 seed beads threaded together, creating a scalloped effect.

Accessories

Beaded shoes

Beaded shoes have been in fashion overseas for many years. They come into vogue periodically.

To embroider a pair of glamorous shoes, you need a pair of shoes covered with fabric to bead onto. Many shoemakers are able to do this. Another technique is to carefully glue each bead in place, but a little patience is needed for this.

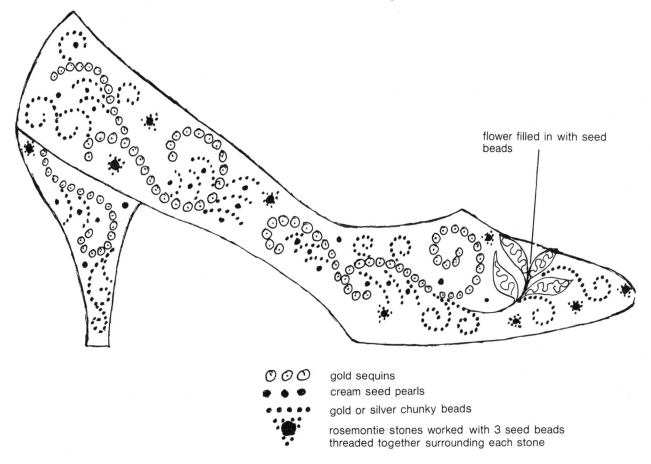

flower filled in with seed beads

⟨⟩ ⟨⟩ ⟨⟩	gold sequins
● ● ●	cream seed pearls
• • • • •	gold or silver chunky beads
(rosemontie stone symbol)	rosemontie stones worked with 3 seed beads threaded together surrounding each stone

Beaded evening shoe

Heritage evening bag

Plate 27

This glamorous drawstring evening bag features an Indian design.

You will need

Black velvet or a heavy satin (size of finished bag 22 cm deep × 19 cm across—allow for seams)
Size 1 gold bugle beads (all gold beads 9 carat gold lined)
Size 2 gold bugle beads
Gold seed beads
Bronze seed beads
16 large orange beads
22 jade-coloured beads the same size
Black silk for lining
Black cord for the top drawstring
Vilene for the interfacing

Method

1. Tack the interfacing onto the fabric. Mark the size of the bag with a tacking thread. Trace design onto the bag.

2. Bead the outline of the design with size 1 gold bugle beads sewn onto the fabric one at a time with whip stitch. Sew one large bead in the centre of each pattern motif using double thread, twice. Alternate the colours of the large beads.

3. Thread together 7 gold seed beads and sew these looped fashion four times around the centre bead. Sew another set of loops, threading 9 beads four times, making a double looped edge. From the centre bead thread 7 gold seed beads together, and sew them outwards to lay flat on the fabric. Repeat 16 times around, filling the small spaces between the gold lines with lines of 5 bronze seed beads. This forms a centre flower. (See sketch.)

4. At each point of the design, sew a size 2 gold bugle bead five times (as shown in sketch). Thread 6 gold seed beads together and sew each side of the bugle bead to form a tiny flower.

After completing all the beading sew the seams together by hand, matching the beading design.

The lining is then cut the same size as the outer bag. Sew together firmly around the top opening of the bag. As this bag has no frame, crochet a looped band about 4 cm wide and sew this firmly to the top of the bag. Thread cord through.

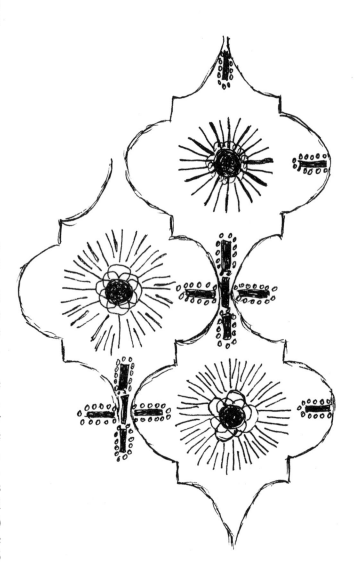

Heritage evening bag, Indian design

70

Embroidered belt

Plate 2

The tambour technique was used for this glamorous
evening belt popular in the 1930s.

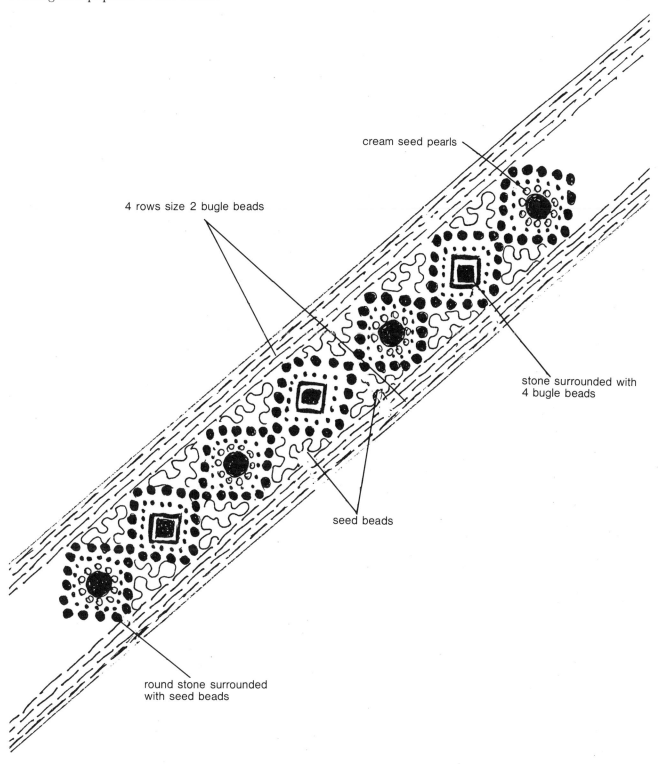

cream seed pearls

4 rows size 2 bugle beads

stone surrounded with
4 bugle beads

seed beads

round stone surrounded
with seed beads

Suppliers

All the beads, sequins, pearls and trimmings shown in this book can be purchased from:

Photios Bros Pty Limited
66 Druitt Street
Sydney NSW 2000
(02) 267 1428

Comprehensive ranges of beads and findings are also carried by:

Bead Co. of Australia*
497 Elizabeth Street
Surry Hills 2010
(02) 318 2775

Beads Galore Pty Ltd
25a Playfair Street
The Rocks, Sydney 2000
(02) 247 5946

Beadz of Hurstville
324 Forest Road
Hurstville 2220
(02) 580 4923

We've Got The Beads
577 Elizabeth Street
Redfern NSW 2016
(02) 319 3355

Stadia Handcrafts
85 Elizabeth Street
Paddington 2021
(02) 328 7900

The Bead Co. of Victoria*
336 Smith Street
Collingwood 3066
(03) 419 0636

Maria George Pty Ltd
179 Flinders Lane
Melbourne 3000
(03) 650 1151
(03) 650 4117

Glamour 'N' Glitter Pty Ltd
49 Atkinson Street
Chadstone 3148
(03) 563 1300

Bead & Trimming Co.*
69 Elizabeth Street
Brisbane 4000
(07) 221 1315

The Bead Shop*
190 Goodwood Road
Millswood 5034
(08) 373 1296

Tanami Garden Centre
Paterson Street
Tennant Creek 0860
(089) 62 2809

*indicates mail order service available.

Many department stores and haberdashers also carry a range of beads.